What Was It Like?™
GEORGE WASHINGTON

by Lawrence Weinberg
illustrated by Alex Bloch

Longmeadow Press

Published by Longmeadow Press
201 High Ridge Road, Stamford, CT 06904

ANGEL
ENTERTAINMENT INC.

Manufactured in the United States of America.

I suppose you've heard the story about me as a child going up to my father and saying, "I cannot tell a lie. I chopped down that cherry tree!"

Well, a parson named Weems made up that story after folks started to call me "the father of our country." He did it to teach boys and girls to be as honest as George Washington. It would have been nicer if he had been just a little more honest himself, because I never did chop down that tree!

Everyone has read that I was born in 1732 on a tobacco plantation in Virginia; that in 1775 I became the general who led the revolution to free the thirteen American Colonies from England; and that in 1789 I became the first President of the United States. But sometimes they think about me only as a name in history books, and not as a man! It's no wonder that I'm made to look so stiff and stuffy in all those paintings and statues of "the father of our country."

But when I was a little boy, I loved what other children love—running, jumping, playing and swimming in our little river with the big name, the Rappahannock! I'm sure that you, too, would have been excited about the candy and presents that came up our little river on a sailing ship about once a year—all the way across the ocean

from England! My younger brothers and sisters and I would run down the hill from our house to the dock. The captain would give us the gifts my father had ordered for us. If we stayed out of the way while the barrels of our plantation's tobacco were being loaded aboard, we could even walk around the deck of the ship! So you see, I knew how to have fun, even though there were some people who kept noticing what a serious lad I seemed to be. To be honest, as I was growing up, I tried very hard to look serious!

This was important to me, especially since my father died when I was only eleven years old. I was the oldest boy—except for my two grown half brothers, who didn't live with us—so I became the man of the family.

Not that my mother treated me seriously, no matter how serious I tried to look. She didn't let me have any real spending money to use when I wanted to take the ferry across the Rappahannock to the little town of Fredericksburg. She wouldn't let me help run the farm, either—not even after I grew up! And she had such a terrible temper that my friends were more afraid of her than of their own parents!

I always believed in honoring my parents, but I think you can now see one of the reasons why I became very restless at home. I was glad to be outdoors as much as possible, galloping off on my horse, flying over ditches and fences with the wind rushing past my face. It blew away all my unhappiness, and I felt free! People used to say I was the best rider they had ever seen. I don't know if they were just being kind, but I suppose it's easy to be good at what you love to do.

There were other things I enjoyed, too, like running rapids on the river in an Indian bark canoe and wrestling with other boys, although it was much too easy for me to win. I hope you don't think I'm boasting about my strength. I tried all my life not to brag about anything. But you see, wrestling and going long distances without rest or sleep came easily to me. I took after my father, who was a giant of a man and as strong as a bull.

Of course, I had to study when I was a boy, and I can't pretend *that* always came easily to me. But I worked pretty hard at it. Believe it or not, geometry was one of my favorite subjects. I liked it because it was practical. A person could use it to help measure the size of different pieces of land. Surveyors did that when they were setting aside plots of land for farming and other uses.

Surveying sounded like just the right job for me. For one thing, it was outdoor work. And for

another, even a young assistant surveyor could make enough money so that he wouldn't have to ask his mother for any!

My half brother Lawrence helped me get started in the surveying business. Lawrence and I had different mothers—his mother had died a long time ago—and he was away at school in England until I was eight years old. Of course, I had heard a lot about him, but almost as soon as he came back from England, he sailed off to war. He went to help the British Army attack an island owned by the Spanish.

My brother wasn't an English soldier, though. He was a major in the Virginia militia. When he came back from the war, he had a terrible story to tell. But it was not about the Spanish—who were supposed to be our enemies—but about the British general who led the attack! This man looked down on anyone who came from the Colonies, and he treated the Virginians much worse than he did his own soldiers. When his Redcoats got terribly sick with yellow fever, they were taken care of, while our men were often left to die.

Lawrence never forgave the English commanding general for his neglect. But he did admire the

Admiral of the Fleet that had carried the troops. His name was Vernon, which is why Lawrence renamed his beautiful plantation, Mount Vernon. As often as I could get away from home, Lawrence let me come to stay with him at Mount Vernon. When I was sixteen, he let me move into the house!

Lawrence was a busy and important man in Virginia. But he took time to be with me, to make me feel wanted, and to help me in any way he could. He told me a lot about England and the Appleby School, where he and my other half brother, and my father before them, had studied. My mother said she couldn't afford to send me to the Appleby School, but that was all right. Lawrence could teach me what he had learned there.

Things became especially nice at Mount Vernon after Lawrence married Anne Fairfax. Her father ran the greatest plantation in all of Virginia. The plantation really belonged to his cousin, who was a British lord! The whole Fairfax family took a liking to me. When old Lord Fairfax came to visit from England, they told him that I had a way with horses. He asked me to go fox hunting with him. Since chasing foxes was just about the most important thing in his life, Lord Fairfax saw a lot of me. He heard, too, that I was good at surveying. One day, he saw me measuring my brother's turnip fields. "E'gad!" he said, looking at my drawing, "You do it with such care, George, that you could be laying out an entire town!"

Later on, he told me he had hired a very fine surveyor to do a big job for him in the western wilderness. How would I like it, he asked, if he made me the man's assistant? I can't tell you how excited I was!

We set out in early March, 1748, although that meant crossing a river still swollen from the snow melting in the mountains. We couldn't have waited until later in the spring, because all the leaves would be on the trees by then and it would be harder to see distances. We swam our horses across the fast-moving river and rode the narrow trails that led up the slopes of the Blue Ridge Mountains.

We were in forests where the deer and the bears saw very few human beings. We had brought some food along, but hunted wild turkeys with our long guns whenever we could. I was a good shot, and one day I got a gobbler that must have weighed over twenty pounds. We ate well then!

It was a long, hard journey. At last, we came down the other side of the mountain range into the huge valley of the Shenandoah River. Beneath us stretched the land Lord Fairfax wanted us to survey, a land filled with fields and forests. The land was a gift that had been made to his family many years before by the King of England. What a gift—over five million acres!

It was hard and tiring work, drawing maps for smaller parcels so that Lord Fairfax could sell them off to farmers and settlers who wanted to come west from Pennsylvania. Each day, after we finished our surveying, we'd build a campfire. We'd hold forked sticks over the fire to cook our food, then eat and go to sleep as soon as the sun went down.

One day, a band of about thirty very fierce-looking Indian braves came towards our little camp. One of them was even proudly carrying somebody's freshly cut scalp! We had our rifles handy, but could never have fought so many of them. As it turned out, though, we weren't the enemy who had caused the Indians to put on their war paint. They were coming from a battle they'd had with another tribe, and saw no reason to attack us.

We made friends with the Indians, and our interpreter asked them to show us a war dance. They made a circle around a big bonfire. Then

their best dancer jumped into the ring. The others followed him one at a time. While they danced, two musicians began to play. One Indian brave pounded his hands on a drum made out of a pot that was half-filled with water. The other brave rattled a gourd filled with stones.

We all had a good time that night. That was more than I could say about the meetings we had with some white settlers we later found on Lord Fairfax's land. They were farmers, but Lord Fairfax would have called them rascals and squatters! They spoke only Dutch, but we didn't need to understand their words to see what they thought of us!

I was angry at the farmers for scowling and waving their fists at us as we worked. But I was very young then, and also very loyal to Lord Fairfax. I wasn't thinking about what it meant to these folks when they saw what we were doing with our measuring tools. One day they might be told that they had no right to stay there. Then they would have to leave their homes and give up the fields they had cleared and planted. And all because the King of England had long ago given a piece of paper to someone who had never even set foot on the land!

It was a full month before we returned from the

Shenandoah Valley. Lord Fairfax was so pleased that soon I was getting other surveying work. This took me back to the wilderness again and again — exploring the land, camping out, and then finding some kind family who'd let me spend the night with them. More often than not, there would be no proper beds in their one-room log cabins. We'd all lie on beds of straw on the floor, or on a bearskin rug in front of the fire. On a cold night, the wind would howl through the chinks in the log walls. The happiest person was always the one who slept closest to the fireplace!

It was a good life for a boy. During the three years I worked at it, I grew stronger and more able to take care of myself. I made enough money to support myself, and even had some left over to save. And I was proud of being good at what I did.

But there was one thing, I have to admit, that I was not so handy at—that was getting along with girls when I was back home. I suppose I was more used to the wilderness than I was to civilized society. So I took dancing lessons and went to parties whenever I could. But that didn't help me much. For one thing, I was never much of a talker. And for another, I was a little shy, especially since I was so much bigger and taller than anyone else. There was also that grave expression I had gotten used to keeping on my face. I just couldn't get rid of it!

One of my dreams was to own a farm. I put aside every penny I could. As soon as I had enough, I'd go out and buy land that I could work myself. And someday, yes, someday, I might even have a Mount Vernon of my own, and a wonderful wife, as my brother Lawrence did!

However, Lawrence was not able to enjoy his happiness for long. He came down with a terrible disease called consumption (tuberculosis). He coughed a lot and grew weaker and weaker. I couldn't bear to think that he might die. I took him first to a warm spring in the mountains, but the weather there was so foggy and damp that he wasn't helped at all.

We decided to try something else. I bundled him aboard a ship and sailed with him to the Island of Barbados, where the weather was very warm. There were terrible storms at sea. When we finally reached the island, my brother only grew worse. He had to go back home. It wasn't long before we buried him there.

Lawrence had been more like a father to me than a brother and his death was very hard for me to bear. He did a very nice thing, though, and left me with a new home — Mount Vernon! It now

belonged to his widow, but Anne moved away and let me rent it. Afterwards, it became mine completely—the home I kept for the rest of my life. I don't know what I loved it for more—its beauty, or the memories of Lawrence that it always held for me.

Lawrence left me something else, too—the dream of becoming a soldier. I thought it was my duty to see to it that another Washington took Lawrence's place. I had never forgotten the excitement of watching him go off to fight the Spanish. Young boys often fall in love with glittering uniforms and marching bands. The truth is that I never stopped being excited by them. During the time that I was having trouble at home with my mother, I dreamed of faraway adventures. I wanted to win the cheers and hurrahs of the people of Virginia, and even of the king!

I ought to tell you something about the way people thought of war back then. Nowadays, everyone agrees that war is a terrible thing. Later in my life, I came to think so myself. But when I was young, and for many centuries before I was born, war was thought to be very glamorous and exciting!

People often wanted to have a war. It made them forget how difficult or how boring their lives sometimes were. And what better way was there for a young man to prove his bravery? Fewer soldiers got hurt in most of those wars, too, because armies weren't nearly as big. And though some men did get killed while they were still young, not many people in my time lived to be more than thirty-five or forty years old anyway! So, they might have thought, why not die a hero?

This was no time for shyness. I talked to a lot of important people who had known Lawrence. They spoke to the royal governor on my behalf. And in my brother's honor, Lieutenant Governor Dinwiddie made me a major. For a nineteen-year-old who was looking for adventure, I had gotten a uniform at the perfect time. Big trouble was brewing way out west in the great Ohio Valley.

About seventy years earlier, a Frenchman called La Salle had come down by canoe from Canada and the Great Lakes to explore the territory. The French were the owners of Canada then, and their trappers used to come south in the spring to trade with the Indians for furs. Because of this, the King of France had been saying for a long time that all the land from Canada in the north to the Gulf of Mexico in the south belonged to him. But the French hadn't really done much about claiming the land, except to set up some trading

posts. So the English hadn't paid too much attention.

But now came the news that the French were building forts along the Ohio River. The King of England began to get worried. If this were allowed to go on, then his American Colonies would no longer be able to expand west! Our governor thought it was a terrible thing, too, for business. He belonged to a company that wanted the king's permission to sell some of that same land to our settlers.

The king's ministers sent orders to the governor to tell the French to get out of the Ohio Valley if they didn't want war. To deliver the warning, the governor needed somebody who knew how to travel through the wilderness. So I volunteered! It was going to be a one thousand mile journey to the main French fort near Lake Erie, and an early winter was on its way. Without wasting a single moment after I got my orders, I galloped off.

On the way, I hired a French-speaking Dutchman named Braam to interpret for me. Then I found a frontiersman named Gist to guide me, and four other helpers. Soon we were struggling with our horses through a furious storm of rain, sleet and snow.

On we went, climbing over the Blue Ridge

Mountains and down into the Shenandoah Valley. Our pack horses had trouble moving in the heavy snow. It took us a full week to go seventy-five miles! Then, at last, we came to the cabin of a friendly Indian trader. He gave us some very bad news. The French had told the Indians terrible stories about the English. Three tribes were already on the warpath against us!

Yet part of my mission had been to make allies for England with any friendly Indians we could find along the way. We traveled for days along Indian trails until we came close to Lake Erie. There was the fort, with its cannons pointing straight at us. We saw no one, and heard nothing but silence. Then suddenly, the gates swung open and French officers came out to invite us inside for dinner!

Later, I saw the commander and gave him my message from the king. We were very polite to each other. He was so friendly that he even let me wander around the fort. I liked that because it gave me a chance to see how strong they were. I would report all that I saw to the governor.

When I got back, the governor said many kind words about how I had handled my mission. He promoted me to lieutenant colonel, and not long afterwards sent me out once again. A small group of Virginians had started to build a fort at a place called the Forks, on the Ohio River. In the spring of 1754, we heard that a group of French soldiers was going to come down the river in canoes to attack them. I was ordered to hurry up and march my troops to their defense.

After begging and borrowing supplies, I finally got together about one hundred and sixty men. Not one of them had the training necessary to stand up to the French soldiers. But then, neither did I. We had no choice, however, so we set out for the Forks of the Ohio River, and in order to protect ourselves from ambush, ended up launching a sneak attack on the French!

We lost the battle, and I had to surrender to the French. As we traveled home with our wounded, my heart was breaking. So many good Virginian lads had come to grief because of me. The price was high, but I had been taught a lesson about this kind of war that I would never forget. However, it began to look as if I would never have the chance to put the lesson I'd learned to use. When the King of England found out what was written in the peace treaty with France that I had been forced to sign, he was furious. It said that I admitted having had no right to make that surprise attack when I was on the way to the Forks!

This made it look as if it was the English who had started the war! As a punishment, I lost my command. I went back to my plantation thinking that my life as a soldier was over forever.

But there is one thing about the future. You never know what is going to happen. By the next summer, everything had changed. A British general named Braddock was coming over from England with two regiments of Redcoats. He was going to march them to the Ohio River and beat the French once and for all. He invited me to come along with him as an advisor. He knew I had lost a battle, but all soldiers lose battles. I still had more experience in marching troops through the wilderness than anyone else.

I liked General Braddock right away. There were many wonderful things about him, although he had one major fault. He asked for advice, and then didn't pay attention to it. He marched his Redcoats straight ahead without bothering to make sure that there was no one hiding behind the trees on either side. Enemy marksmen opened fire from their hiding places and killed most of our troops, including General Braddock.

This British defeat was a terrible thing for the Colonies. For a long time afterwards, England sent no more troops. The war with the French had spread to Europe, and the British meant to keep most of their army there.

Meanwhile, we colonists had to defend our settlers against the French rifle and the Indian tomahawk. It was a very hard time, but it was a time that helped us to start changing as a people. We were beginning to stop thinking of ourselves as Virginians and Pennsylvanians and Marylanders, and so on. We started thinking of ourselves as Americans.

I had wanted to become a hero. Well, now I was thought of as one. Many people said that Braddock would have won if he had listened to me. They'd also heard stories about how I had tried to calm the troops. They said that if it hadn't been for me, even more soldiers would have been killed.

It was nice that people spoke highly of young George Washington, but what I really cared about was that our people were suffering. I had a chance to do something about all that suffering when I was made commander in chief of Virginia's army. It was a fine title, but our forces were very small and the enemy knew all the secrets of surprise. Farms and homes were attacked and burned.

Some people fled the frontier at the slightest rumor that Indians might be near. Half of the time, we were chasing false alarms. At least we managed to head off some of the raids. We helped the Colonies hold on until the British began to win battles in Europe and in Canada.

By now I had stopped thinking about the glories of war. I just wanted it to end. I wanted to go back to farming on my beautiful plantation at Mount Vernon. And I wanted a wife and family.

The war dragged on and on until, finally, the French were defeated. They had lost Canada to the British. When they disappeared from our west, the Indian tribes that had fought beside them could not stand alone. The terrible raids were over.

Our Colonial lads had hardly returned to their farms and towns before I married Martha Custis, a pretty widow. She was bright and good-hearted. So were her two children, Patsy and Jacky, whom I came to love as if they were my own. I never had any other children.

The years passed. We raised our children and watched them play. We had parties for our friends and went visiting. We grew tobacco and wheat, raised cattle and race horses and hunting dogs. And we were happy.

But there was trouble growing between the Colonies and England. The English had borrowed a lot of money to spend on the war with the French. Laws were passed in Parliament to make the Colonies help pay some of it back. Many colonists were still angry over how little help we had actually gotten during the war. Besides, the British did not allow us to elect any of the men in the Parliament who made those laws.

The British said we were ungrateful. We said they were unfair. "No taxation without representation!" we cried.

But this quarrel was about more than taxes. We colonists felt that the English weren't treating us as equals. My brother Lawrence had been angry about that during the war against Spain. I had seen some of the same thing, too, during the war with the French. Many English officers would not follow my orders, even though I was in charge. Sometimes they would not even allow their Redcoats to work alongside our own lads, clearing the trails and pulling heavy loads.

We colonists had learned something about defending ourselves during that war. We did not expect to be treated this way, and we said so. One of the best-remembered examples of this would soon become known as the "Boston Tea Party."

This was no party, but a gathering of people who tried to protest the high tax on tea by dumping whole crates of it into Boston Harbor!

I didn't care for that way of showing dissatisfaction. I never believed in destroying other people's property. But when the king sent ships and troops to take over Boston, I thought that was outrageous. A meeting of all the Colonies was called in Philadelphia to decide what to do about it. The Virginia Assembly sent me. I hoped the king would change his mind when he received our petition. If he did, we would remain his loyal subjects, but if he didn't, then we'd have to fight for our rights.

The war began with Paul Revere's ride on the night of April 18, 1775. Revere rode from Boston to warn the people of Concord and Lexington that the Redcoats were coming to their towns. The Redcoat commander had sent his troops to seize arms and gunpowder that he believed some of the colonists had stored there. Farmers and townspeople took up their muskets and hurried from their homes. There was a battle. Men died on both sides.

Someone said the first shot was like a shot that had been heard around the world. Freedom was going to have to be fought for. Another Continen-

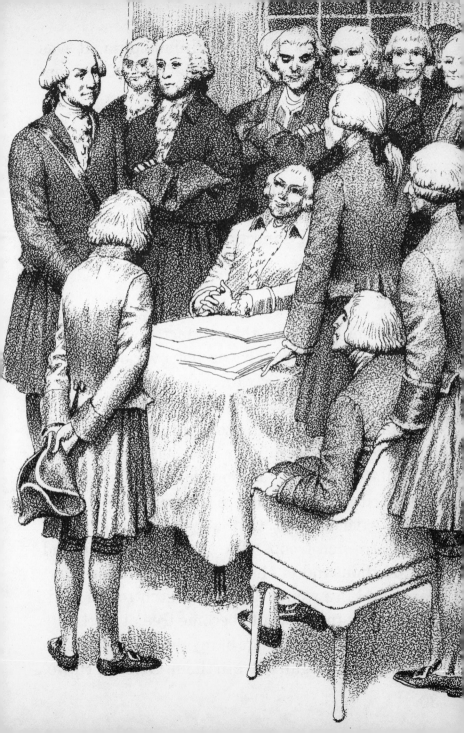

tal Congress was called in Philadelphia. It was time to pick a Commander in Chief of the Continental Army.

I went to that meeting of the Continental Congress and said very little, as usual. Everybody wanted me to be elected Commander in Chief. Mr. Adams of Massachusetts said that I had "great experience and abilities in military matters." And a man from Connecticut said that I was "...no harum-scarum fellow, but sober, steady and calm!"

The truth is, that I expected to lead the army, if we could pull one together. In fact, I was already wearing my uniform. I was not overjoyed, however, at the prospect of war.

Still, I set out right away to join the brave men who had fought at Lexington. On my way, I heard about the Battle of Bunker Hill. "General, we lost the hill," I was told, "but our men held it against three British attacks before they retreated."

That gave me hope. Ordinary folks had stood up to well-trained troops. They had not broken and run. A thousand of the English had fallen. Perhaps the king would decide to listen to our petitions now—and we could become free at last!

I joined the beginnings of my new army outside of Boston and began to train them. General Howe, the British commander in Boston, hadn't expected anything like this! Why these riffraff colonists were behaving as if they had a real army! Loading his men aboard the ships in the harbor, he sailed away.

The Colonies went wild with their first big victory. Even I hoped for a while that all the trouble might soon be over. But that was just wishful thinking. Later we learned that the British Navy was bringing more troops over from England. When it did, General Howe would land them all in New York City!

I marched my new troops there to prepare for General Howe's invasion. But they landed an army that was so huge we could never have conquered it—over thirty thousand well-trained men!

Now we knew what we were up against. But when my soldiers heard about the Declaration of Independence, they cheered anyway! Some of them rushed into a park, took hold of a statue of King George, and melted it down for bullets. Well, we needed every one of those bullets. We were a poor army—poor in equipment, poor in training, and poor in numbers. And the English meant to destroy us once and for all.

I was beginning to see how we had to fight this

war. We had to do it almost as if we were Indians. We had to stay away from battles out in the open where there were too many against us, and use the tactic of surprise whenever we could. We might not win this war, but maybe we could keep from losing it! If we could hold out long enough, I prayed, the British might grow weary. Then they would stop sending their own young men to die three thousand miles across the ocean. Until then, I had to look for a special kind of victory—keeping my army together even when we lost battles.

Once in a while, I was able to give the soldiers something to cheer their souls—a battle we could win! I remember a bitterly cold Christmas night. We were on one side of the Delaware River, across from Trenton, New Jersey, where many enemy troops were stationed. Twenty-four hundred of us climbed into rowboats. Speaking only in whispers, we pushed aside the floating chunks of ice as we made our way to the other side. The enemy soldiers were too sleepy or drunk to know what was happening. The battle went swiftly, and one thousand men surrendered!

These victories made our spirits soar, but they weren't enough to defeat the great forces of the

British Empire. The fighting went on and on. Our men were in rags as they marched through the snow with bare and bleeding feet to the hillsides of Valley Forge. There, in that freezing place, we camped. But the chill in the soldiers' bodies was not nearly as bad as the chill that was in their hearts, for we were so very nearly beaten.

The men were braver than brave. In spite of everything—poor food, no pay and a nearly hopeless war—they persisted. Somehow, we managed to get through the winter. Another part of my army further north had won a tremendous victory. A British force sweeping from Canada had been beaten at Saratoga, New York, and the English general had surrendered!

Because of this, there was even better news. Benjamin Franklin had been in France for years, trying to get the French to help us against their old enemy, England. But King Louis XVI had held back. He wanted to see if the Americans stood a chance of winning. Now Franklin had a victory to show him, and France went to war for our side!

Even with French help, three more years of struggle lay ahead. But at last there was a great battle at Yorktown, Virginia. French troops, joining mine, attacked on land. A fleet of French ships kept the British from escaping by water as they

had in Boston. On October 19, 1781, General Cornwallis handed me his sword. England gave up the war, and the United States of America was free at last!

Everyone could see now that the war was coming to an end, and that we had won. All of my men rejoiced, but they had fought and bled for years without having been paid the money that was promised to them. If they went home now, many of them would not have a penny in the world. Yet the states had not given Congress the power to raise the needed funds. During the war, there had been mutinies among some of the soldiers. The officers were angry, as well. Many of them began to talk about using the army to force Congress and the states to come up with the promised money. Others thought that it would be a splendid thing to bring down Congress altogether and crown me George the First, King of America!

People like to think of George Washington, the man with the serious expression, as a man who never lost his temper. Well, that was just about as true as Parson Weems's story about the cherry tree! It enraged me that anyone would dare to think that I had led this revolution against one tyrant in order to make myself another one!

But the threat of an officers' rebellion was something I would have to handle more calmly. I called a meeting of my officers and started to reason with them. My heart sank as I realized that they were angry with me. The men I had led in battle, and whom I loved, no longer thought that I was on their side. Of course I was—I just did not believe that we should destroy this new government of the people by using the army to bully the Congress. If we did that even once, I thought, America would be doomed. That would be a far greater injustice than the one from which they now suffered.

When I saw that they weren't listening to me, I stopped speaking. I didn't know what to say. I thought of reading them a letter sent to me by a congressman. I reached into my coat for my glasses. As I put them on, I realized that none of the officers had ever seen me wearing glasses.

"Gentlemen," I said "you will permit me to put on my spectacles, for I have not only grown gray, but almost blind in the service of my country."

Suddenly, everything changed in the meeting place. There were sobs and silent bursts of tears. The hall was filled with crying men. Through the mist in my own eyes, I could see the love on the faces of each and every one of these men.

Eight-and-a-half years had passed. I finally went home to Martha and the children and Mount Vernon. I thought this was the end of my service to my fellow countrymen. I was fifty years old, but I felt older. The struggle had tired me. I wanted to be a peaceful farmer and nothing more. I bought fertilizer to improve the soil and experimented with new seeds and fresh crops. I built a new kind of barn and hired a farm manager who had been trained in scientific farming.

Still, I couldn't stop thinking about what was happening to our country. We desperately needed to improve our form of government. And now there was going to be a convention in Philadelphia to write a Constitution.

I was asked to go to the convention. With a new Constitution, I thought, we might finally have a government that could actually raise money, through taxes, to pay its soldiers. The old government hadn't been able to do that, which was why the brave lads who had served under me had gone hungry. I knew there were still many people who wouldn't want the federal government to be stronger. I wanted the states to be strong, too, but above all, America had to be unified.

When I arrived at the Constitutional Convention, bells rang out and guns saluted me. Brave young Alexander Hamilton, who had fought beside me, was there, as were twenty-nine other men whom I'd commanded in the war. Small wonder, I suppose, that I was asked to preside over the discussions. But this time I was not going to order anybody around. With brilliant men like James Madison and Benjamin Franklin there to speak, I saw no reason why I should be telling everyone what to do.

There was a lot of talking and plenty of arguing in Independence Hall, but finally the Constitution was written. The Constitution had to be ratified by at least nine of the thirteen states. Some of the states insisted that the Constitution must also be amended to include a Bill of Rights. Otherwise, the individual liberties for which we had fought would not be protected. After many debates, the Constitution finally became the law of the land.

Then the call to serve my country came once again. I was home one day in April, 1789, when a messenger arrived to tell me that I had been elected the first President of the United States of America. Again, I would rather have stayed at home and been a planter. There were many other people who had helped to create America—like Thomas Paine, whose writings had stirred the people to dream of freedom. And Jefferson, who had written the Declaration of Independence. If I was to be called the father of our country then perhaps Benjamin Franklin should have been called its grandfather. He, more than anyone, had made the rest of the world understand our struggle and had gotten the help we needed from France. But no greater honor could have been given to any man. When the call came, I had no choice but to accept.

There was no capital city then. I set out on horseback for New York, and Martha followed later. People greeted me all along the way, still calling me "General." I finally crossed into New York City on a sailing barge and took the oath of office.

What shall I say about my first four years as president? There was one very big disappointment. Two political parties began to form, one fighting against the other. My secretary of treasury, Alexander Hamilton, led a group called the Federalists. My secretary of state, Thomas Jefferson, led the other group called the Democratic Republicans. They were both men of great intelligence and they both loved the country. They were entitled to have different ideas about the future of America, but the country was being split in half by these two political parties that only tried to

shout down and beat one another.

If it hadn't been for all of this quarreling, I probably would not have agreed to be nominated for a second term as president. But America was just too young to be torn apart this way. I felt I could help to hold the country together for another four years while it grew stronger.

There was another big problem. War had broken out again between France and England. Jefferson wanted us to help the French, saying that we owed it to them. What's more, they had just had a revolution of their own. Many people agreed with Jefferson. But there were a lot of others, like Hamilton, who thought that the French Revolution had been too bloody. They also felt that we should bury our differences with England—our mother country.

I wanted to keep the United States out of a war between two enemies who had been fighting each other for hundreds of years. I wanted us to mind our own business and build up our own nation. So I signed a proclamation that stated we would not take sides. Many people were disappointed with my decision, but they had not been the commanding general of an army who had seen so many young men die.

I did not even consider running for a third term.

After eight years as president, it was time to go home. In 1797, Martha and I went back to Mount Vernon. And there we remained together in happiness for the rest of our days.

What is it that means the most to me, when I look back over my life? Is it that I managed to hold our army of young farmers and storekeepers together? Is it that I helped this new country to be born? Or is it that when the people wanted to make me a king, I refused? I can only say that I believed in democracy, and I wanted a free people.

In the end, what I most wanted those free people to know about me was that George Washington could always be depended upon to give his best for his country.

The Life and Times of
George Washington

1732 George Washington is born on February 22, on his father's farm at Bridges Creek, near Fredericksburg, Virginia.

1748 George is hired as an assistant surveyor by Lord Fairfax, and journeys through the wilderness to the Shenandoah Valley.

1752 Following the death of his beloved half brother Lawrence, George inherits Mt. Vernon and joins the Virginia militia as an officer.

1754 As a leader of a small force of Virginia militia, George fights the battle that launches the great French and Indian War.

1759 George marries Martha Dandridge Custis, a widow with two children. He raises the children as his own.

1774 George attends the first Continental Congress on September 5.

1775 The clash between British Redcoats and Colonial "Minutemen" at Lexington and Concord in Massachussetts, sets off the American Revolution. Meeting of Second Continental Congress is held, and on June 15, 1775, George is unanimously chosen to be Commander in Chief of all revolutionary forces.

1776　The Declaration of Independence is signed on July 4. On Christmas day, in a surprise attack, George crosses the Delaware to overwhelm an encampment of mercenary soldiers in Trenton, New Jersey. The next day, while dodging the main British Army, he defeats three British Regiments at Princeton.

1777-　After the loss of Philadelphia, George's
1778　forces camp for the winter in Valley Forge, Pennsylvania, under terrible conditions. France enters the war on America's side.

1781　British General Cornwallis surrenders at Yorktown, Virginia, on October 19. This signals America's victory over England.

1787　The Constitutional Convention meets in Philadelphia, and after four months produces a Constitution.

1789　On March 30, George Washington takes the oath of office as the first President of the United States. He serves a second term and retires in March, 1797.

1799　On December 14, George Washington dies quietly in his bed after a short illness.